The Châte
de V

Jean Chapelot,
Centre national de l

y Louis VII, the manor at Vincennes served, from the reign of his great-grandson Saint Louis, as the favoured residence of 13th- and 14th-century French monarchs, rivalled only by the Palais de la Cité in Paris. Vincennes became a royal residence; the image thus formed would leave an impression on France until the 17th century. A second characteristic of the site developed when, shortly after the mid-14th century, Jean le Bon [John II the Good] and above all his son Charles V built the keep and castle enceinte. This magnificent fortified residence also doubled as a place of refuge for the sovereigns during troubled or difficult periods until the mid-17th century.

From the Revolution to World War II, every political regime maintained the castle because of its proximity to Paris, its scale and its wall and moat protection, defending both the capital and its government. After the last war, once the army, navy and air-force history departments were installed, the monument was opened to the public. Its eight centuries of existence, constantly at the centre of history, have made it one of the great memorial sites of France.

The keep and its enceinte♦, seen from the east

♦**Enceinte:**
The main enclosure of a castle or fortress, surrounded by a wall and/or ditch or moat.

Visitors are struck by its massive size, but the highest keep in Europe is not limited merely to that aspect. The only residence of a medieval monarch surviving in France, it is also a remarkably well-preserved construction of outstanding quality, erected in record time between 1361 and 1369, using exceptional architectural techniques. Its decoration, both interior and exterior, is of the highest interest, exceedingly rich from an iconographic point of view.
French sovereigns resided there from the 14th to the 16th centuries; two died on the premises. After the 16th century, however, kings were

replaced by prisoners of whom certain, through their personality or their writings, were to give the keep a second lease of life in the history of France. They were often eminent personages: the future Henri IV in 1574, the Great Condé in 1650 or Fouquet (Louis XIV's Minister of Finance) in 1661, men of letters, for example Diderot, the Comte de Mirabeau or the Marquis de Sade in the later 1700s, Charles X's ministers in 1830, or Republicans such as Raspail in 1848.
Few French medieval edifices have remained for as long at the centre of history or proved as significant as the keep at Vincennes.

The restoration of the keep was completed in 2006. Its enceinte will be restored at a later date.

Paris and its eastern outskirts during Charles V's reign. The castle was located on the forest periphery, enclosed by a wall since the late 12th century. Drawing by Jean-Claude Golvin.

The royal manor: 12th-14th centuries

Located on a plateau to the east of Paris, the forest of Vincennes had belonged to the Bishop of Paris, probably since the time of the Merovingians. In 1037 Henri I, King of France, granted common rights in this forest to the abbey of Saint-Maur-des-Fossés, demonstrating that part of the wood had by then passed into the hands of the Capetians. However this fact does not signify that a royal residence already existed there.
Several phenomena account for the creation of a royal residence at Vincennes towards the end of Louis VII's reign (1137-1180), when that sovereign signed a deed there (1178). They include the enhanced role played by Paris, but also the presence of the forest and the possibilities it offered for hunting, the proximity of two former Roman roads (leading from Paris to Sens via the bridge at Charenton and from Paris to Lagny along the Marne valley) and the nearby waterway network allowing the circulation of people and provisions along the Seine and the Marne rivers. Vincennes was, however, still merely a secondary residence: Louis VII, Philippe II Auguste (1180-1223) and Louis VIII (1223-1226) stayed there only occasionally.

A prime residence for Louis IX

Louis IX (1226-1270), on the contrary, with over sixty sojourns, made Vincennes his most frequented residence after the Palais de la Cité in Paris. He bestowed on the manor a new status and importance, maintained by the monarchs until the early 15th century. The nature of acts proclaimed there by the king and of events taking place there attest to the change of use: Vincennes had become not only a place of government and of meetings of the King's Council, but also a family residence where the queen visited, including during the king's absence, with or without their children. That the setting of Vincennes was chosen for various symbolic decisions and events proves the importance of the manor for Saint Louis.
A typical example was the arrival of the Relics of the Passion, purchased in 1237 by the king from the Latin Emperor of the East (Constantinople), Baudouin II de Courtenay. Saint Louis happened to be at Vincennes when, in early August 1239, he was informed that these relics were about to enter his kingdom. He went to Sens where, on 11 August, he solemnly received them in the cathedral. Next he took them to Vincennes whence, on 18 August, the procession left for their entry into the capital. It was for these relics that Saint Louis commissioned the construction of the Sainte-Chapelle♦

♦Sainte-Chapelle: *A palatine reliquary chapel in which important relics are kept, especially those of the Passion. Founded by Saint Louis, King Louis IX, in the heart of the Palais de la Cité, the sovereign's Paris residence and seat of administration, this chapel retains and is commonly known by its original French name the Sainte-Chapelle, whose lower part served as a parish church for neighbouring inhabitants. All the palatine chapels built by Saint Louis or his descendants are modelled upon the capital's Sainte-Chapelle.*

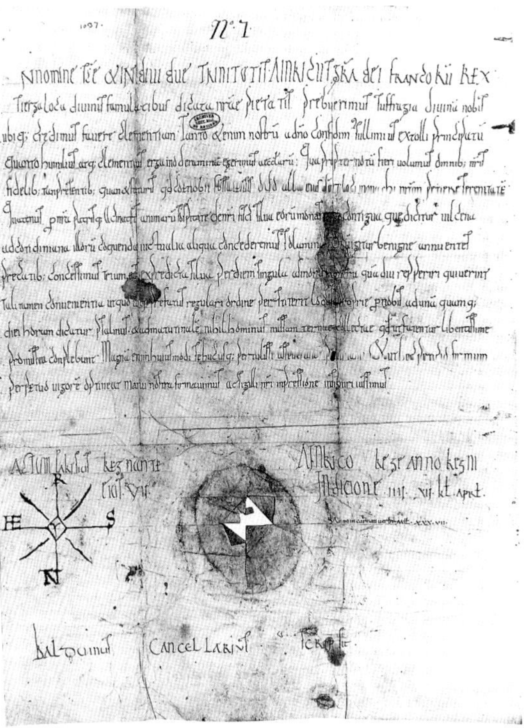

Henri I granted the abbey of Saint-Maur-des-Fossés the right to take three donkey-loads of wood every day from the forest at Vincennes. This rare original document dated 21 March 1037 is the earliest proof that the forest had, at least partially, become the sovereigns' property (Paris, Archives nationales).

(in the Palais de la Cité) inaugurated in 1248. However, a remarkable fact to note is that some of the relics remained at Vincennes: a few thorns from the Crown of Thorns worn by Christ during the Passion and a fragment of the True Cross. Saint Louis deposited some other very rare, exceptional relics in a select number of sites such as his castle at Corbeil or the cathedrals at Senlis and Sens, towns in which he owned residences and very frequently stayed. Thus, by this deposit, Vincennes was assimilated with older and much more prestigious residences.

Another sign lies in the fact that, in the same way as he had chapels constructed in his palaces in Paris, Corbeil, Senlis and Saint-Germain-en-Laye, the king also commissioned a specific palatine reliquary chapel at Vincennes to house the fragments from the Relics of the Passion. In April 1248, shortly before leaving for his first crusade, he installed a resident chaplain there, responsible for celebrating a daily Mass, adopting a practice initiated by Louis VII and Philippe Auguste in the principal royal residences.

Last but not least, when Saint Louis left for the crusades of 1248 and 1270, it was in his manor at Vincennes that he bid his family farewell, after having taken leave of the Parisian population in the cathedral of Notre-Dame and the abbey of Saint-Antoine (in what is now the Marais district).

From the Capetian to the Valois monarchs: more frequent visits

Like Saint Louis, kings from Philippe III (1270-1285) to Charles IV (1322-1328) often resided at Vincennes. There Louis X (1314-1316) was born, lived practically without interruption, and died on 5 June 1316.

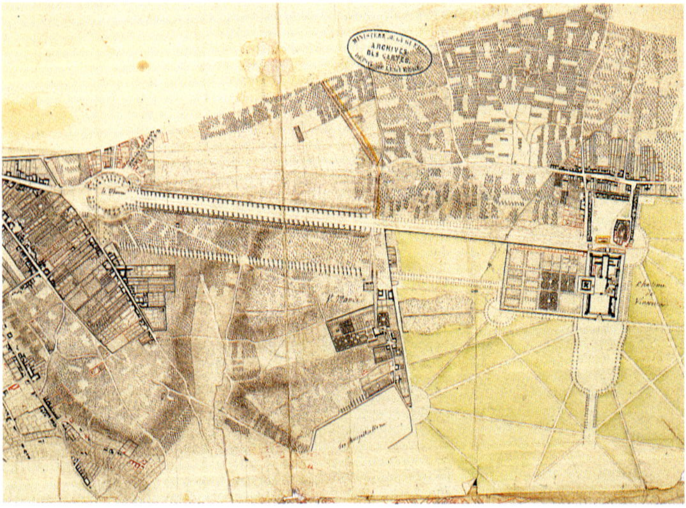

Draft map of the hunts showing the eastern sector of Paris at the end of the *Ancien Régime*. From the north-west corner of the wall enclosing the forest a broad avenue, laid out by Le Vau for the entry of Louis XIV into Paris in 1660, leads to what is now Place de la Nation (Vincennes, Service historique de la Défense).

The first Valois monarch, Philippe VI (1328-1350), favoured Vincennes even more than the kings during preceding reigns. He stayed there at least once a year, sometimes for several months. The manor remained a family residence, particularly appreciated by its female members. The first two queens of the new dynasty, Jeanne de Bourgogne, Philippe VI's wife, and Bonne de Luxembourg, spouse of Jean II le Bon (1350-1364), gave birth between 1320 and 1348 to fourteen children in all, six of whom were born at Vincennes. It was also there that major political decisions were taken, in particular those leading to the outbreak of the Hundred Years War in 1337.

The keep and the towers of the castle enceinte appear above the trees of the forest of Vincennes towards the mid-15th century. Miniature from *Les Très Riches Heures du duc de Berry*, illustration for the month of December (Chantilly, musée Condé).

Saint Louis venerating the Relics of the Passion. This manuscript, which contains the tale of the life and miracles of Saint Louis by Guillaume de Saint-Pathus, was illuminated in Paris circa 1330-1340. It belonged to Charles V (Paris, BnF).

During that era the monarchs lived in the manor house located in the north-east corner of the present castle enceinte.

As far as we know through documentation and above all the excavations undertaken between 1992 and 1996, this manor consisted of buildings erected gradually from the late 12th century. By around the 1350s, they formed an irregular quadrilateral (each side measuring some sixty metres) which housed the kings of France until Charles V installed himself in the keep in 1367-1368. After Vincennes castle's completion in the late 14th century, the manor, handed over to the canons of the chapel, was altered and later demolished. No visible traces remained in the 18th and 19th centuries.

The King of France and the surrounding district

Like the small rural area of La Pissotte (future town of Vincennes), the manor at Vincennes was established in the parish of Montreuil, leading to religious links with that parish church. Charles V, for example, born in the manor on 21 January 1338, was baptised there.

The royal presence must have weighed heavily upon the daily life of inhabitants in neighbouring parishes. On several occasions, in fact, the monarchs purchased land to enlarge the Vincennes forest (for example in 1274-1276 in the direction of Saint-Mandé, then in 1373-1374 to the south-east, towards the Marne), thereby evicting peasants. The latter were subjected to numerous restrictions: the loss of common rights in the forest, the obligation to supply the royal residence when necessary, in particular with hay for the hunt animals, damage or looting suffered when military conflicts of the Hundred Years War raged around the castle, the obligation, by the end of Charles V's reign, to take turns in acting as a lookout in the keep, and the like.

Beyond his own lands, the king extended his hunting activity into neighbouring parishes upon which, therefore, he imposed very strict rules regarding their methods of land use and enclosure. Another heavy burden fell on the inhabitants of Montreuil and La Pissotte: the cost of maintaining the underground pipes and canalised streams supplying water to the royal manor and the Saint-Mandé pond, used for the monarch's fish breeding and as an indispensable watering hole for the rabbits, fallow and roe deer enclosed in the wood, surrounded by a wall from the beginning

Scenes from the life of Saint Louis illustrating a manuscript of *Les Grandes Chroniques de France*, illuminated during Charles V's lifetime and kept in his bedchamber on the second storey of the keep (Paris, BnF).

Philippe VI (top centre) receiving, in 1331, the representatives of Robert d'Artois. Near him, on his right, the kings of Navarre and Bohemia; a little lower, on the left, eight lay peers (Lords temporal), all members of the royal family; on the right, the six ecclesiastical peers (Lords spiritual). The coats of arms placed above them allow the figures to be identified. This *lit de justice*♦ took place at the Louvre, but serves to evoke comparable ones held at Vincennes during the same period (Paris, BnF).

of Philippe Auguste's reign. This last obligation, partially compensated by the exoneration from certain taxes, is documented from 1361 but certainly dates back to Louis IX's reign, at the time when both types of hydraulic installations were set in place. These constraints were abolished only at the time of the Revolution.

Some positive effects mitigated these drawbacks, such as the purchase of white wine (among other products) from the Montreuil and Fontenay vineyards for the Royal Household♦; or the king's and princes' regular alms-giving during important religious or secular ceremonies celebrated in the castle or on the occasion of their royal visits to the church of Montreuil, in particular for the parish feast on 29 June.

♦**Lit de justice:** *A formal session of the deliberations of the high judicial court or Parlement, presided by the king.*

♦***The Royal Household:*** *All those at the king's service, who followed him everywhere.*

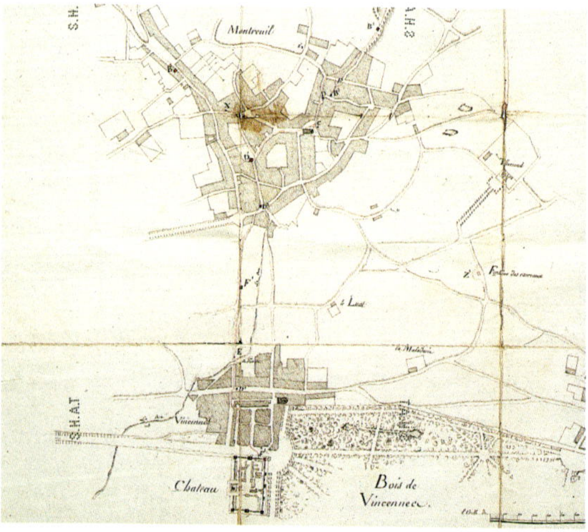

Plan of the hydraulic network supplying the castle in 1816. This Y-shaped network takes the water from springs some 3 km to the north of the castle. Although renovated several times, this plan retains the layout of the first network, set in place before the mid-13th century (Vincennes, Service historique de la Défense).

Saint Louis dispensing justice under an oak tree

Saint Louis, print dating from the second half of the 17th century (Archives of the Société des amis de Vincennes).

Jean, lord of Joinville (circa 1224-1317), one of Saint Louis' most faithful companions during his first crusade in 1248-1254, popularised the monarch's visits to Vincennes. After the king was canonised in 1297, Joinville wrote a *Life of the King*, completed in 1309 and presented to the heir to the throne, the future Louis X. "Many times it happened that in summer [Louis IX] went to sit in the forest of Vincennes after hearing Mass, and leant against an oak tree and had us sit around him; and all those who so desired came to speak to him without hindrance by an usher or anyone else", wrote Joinville. How much truth is there in this image of the king? In the Middle Ages, all judicial authority proceeded from the king, by delegation. At the start of the 13th century, even if the latter no longer dispensed justice like his forebears, still he was at least sometimes present at court sessions. However, in the era of Saint Louis, justice had become the business of specialists trained in law at university. The anecdote recounted by Joinville shows that the king did not pass judgement directly: it was the *maîtres des requêtes*♦ of the Royal Household who attended to it. Joinville meant that the king very closely followed the course of his judicial system. As was often the case for many ceremonies in the Middle Ages, this court of justice could be held in the open air. After Mass, which the king attended each morning, it was traditionally accepted that anyone could approach him easily to present a petition or request. If Joinville set this episode at Vincennes, it was because, at the time of his writing, the memory of the royal saint was intimately associated with the manor.

In fact – and Joinville expresses the matter very clearly – there was no particular oak tree specially assigned for this form of justice, but rather a well-situated spot in the forest near the royal manor. The scene described by Joinville was popularised at the end of the *Ancien Régime* to underline the image of a king who was close to his subjects and one who held his administration firmly in check.

♦Maître des requêtes: *A jurist responsible for making judicial decisions in affairs closely concerning the monarch.*

Saint Louis dispensing justice under an oak tree at Vincennes. Nineteenth-century history books were fond of this scene, as shown by these three engravings (Vincennes, archives municipales).

The castle of Jean II and Charles V

Job on the Dungheap; in the distance, an extremely accurate view of the keep at Vincennes. Miniature from *Les Heures d'Étienne Chevalier*, by Jean Fouquet, circa 1455 (Chantilly, musée Condé).

On 22 April 1361 Jean II le Bon appointed a priest, Jean Goupil, to manage the financing of the new tower he intended to build at Vincennes. By then the Hundred Years War had already lasted a quarter of a century and, on two occasions, the French army had been defeated by the English, in 1346 at Crécy and in 1356 at Poitiers. During this second battle, Jean le Bon was taken prisoner. His oldest son, the future Charles V, then aged eighteen, took over the reins of the kingdom. He had to cope with serious troubles which broke out shortly thereafter: civil insurrection in Paris led by the merchant provost Étienne Marcel in 1357-1358, and a rural rebellion, known as the *Jacquerie* (peasants were nicknamed "*Jacques*") in May-June 1358. After Jean II's release on 25 October 1360 and his solemn entry into Paris on the following 13 December, he drew the necessary conclusion from these events, the necessity of having available, at the gates of Paris, a fortress capable of protecting him against the English, the Parisians and the *Jacques*.

The keep and its enceinte (1361-1370)

The king, the dauphin♦ and their counsellors could not but be aware of the cost of such a project when they decided to build a keep at Vincennes. They chose Vincennes because of the history and prestige of the site, with the aim of creating simultaneously a luxurious royal residence, under security, and a military base at the capital's gates. This multiple programme was totally addressed in the keep and its enceinte.

Written sources and examination of the monument itself allow the chronology of site work to be established. Launched around 1337 by Philippe VI but rapidly halted at foundation level, construction resumed in the spring of 1361. In 1364 the first three storeys of the keep were raised, but the whole was only finished in 1369, although Charles V moved in by 1367 or 1368. Moat excavation around the keep enceinte was underway by 1366, the gatehouse finished in 1369; in 1370-1371 the keep enceinte and abutting buildings were completed. It was thus a very rapidly executed project.

♦Dauphin: *The title borne by the heir to the kingdom of France since the Treaty of Romans which, in 1349, incorporated into the kingdom the Dauphiné [with Grenoble as its capital, a region in east France bordering on Switzerland and Italy].*

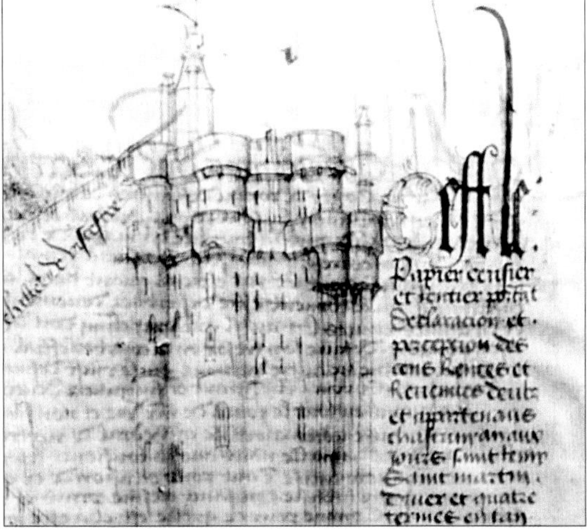

The keep at Vincennes. Pen-and-ink sketch at the top of a *censier* (land rent register) from the seigneury of Bicêtre, 1474 (Paris, Archives nationales).

A substantial garrison

By the end of 1372, even before work on the castle enceinte was undertaken, the keep at Vincennes played a significant role in the kingdom's defence.

The garrison at the time consisted of three categories of military men. The *concierge* or commanding officer and his lieutenant, joined, after 1369, by a captain (responsible for the site) administered the royal residence and the forest. These men, most often from the military, had specialists under their command: first artillery-men, using spring-charged or counterweight weaponry, and then gunners, documented by 1390. The garrison also included ordinary soldiers: in 1370, the captain supported six men-at-arms and six crossbow-men; in 1386 he had six knights and fourteen squires under his orders. In 1370 these men-at-arms were only responsible for the keep but they later guarded the whole of the castle.

With the men-at-arms who followed the king and, since 1369, formed his permanent personal guard, there thus was established a major strength of some seventy to eighty men, probably all well-trained for battle, to protect the castle when the king was in residence.

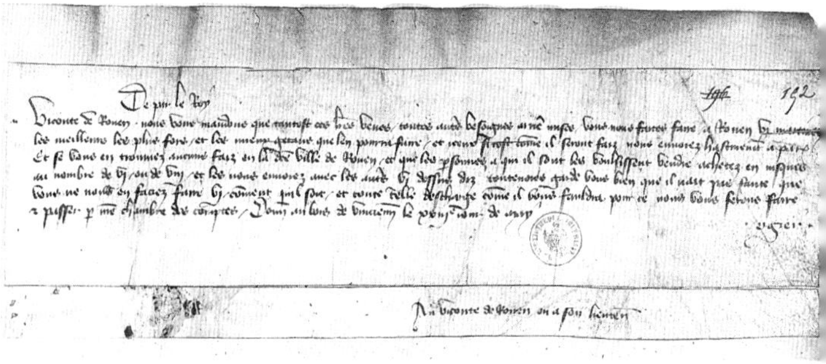

Charles V's mandate of 23 May 1369 ordering the engines of war for the keep terraces. This order implies that the fabric of the keep had been completed (Paris, BnF).

Charles V's castle enceinte (1373-1380)

The years 1367-1370 proved to be a period of great difficulty for the dynasty which, by the Treaty of Brétigny signed in 1360, was deprived of half of its kingdom and was obliged to pay the very heavy ransom promised for freeing Jean II le Bon from his English prison. In 1369 Charles V wished to resume the fight against the English. He installed a heavy fiscal policy which, in 1371, allowed him to set off to war. By the summer of 1372 he had reconquered the greater part of the territory lost in 1360, and his coffers were replenished with taxes created in 1369. So, when at the end of 1372 the King decided to reinforce the keep and its square enceinte structure

Courtly art and politics

Charles V at Porte Saint-Denis, Paris, welcoming his uncle, the Holy Roman Emperor Charles IV, during his official visit to the capital and Vincennes in 1378. Miniature by Jean Fouquet, *Les Grandes Chroniques de France*, 15th century (Paris, BnF).

Upon his accession to the throne, Charles V undertook a series of actions aimed at redressing the kingdom and taking back control of the political domain. A scholarly, well-read king, he had religious and philosophical works translated and called on the best artists to illuminate certain of his manuscripts. A builder king, he entrusted his most important projects to his *maître des œuvres*♦ Raymond du Temple who erected the Château de Vincennes. He gave sculptors the task of decorating his residences, but equally that of directing his image: Charles V was the first monarch portrayed realistically by illuminators, sculptors and painters. Carved effigies of the royal couple were set at the principal points along the east-west route leading from the Louvre to Vincennes via the Bastille. At Vincennes, figures of this type adorned the entries to the gatehouse of the keep and probably those of the three enceinte portal-towers as well as the west front of the palatine reliquary chapel.

Apart from the two thurifer♦ angels at the top of the Tour du Village (the originals, replaced by copies during the 1994 restoration, can be seen in the chapel sacristy), all the free-standing statuary has disappeared from the castle. Nonetheless Vincennes remains the only important testimony to 14th-century royal sculpture. Unfortunately we know nothing about the sculptors who successively worked on the keep and its enceinte (from 1361 to 1370), the Tour du Village and the castle enceinte (from 1373 to 1380), and in the palatine chapel (from the 1390s to the early 15th century).

Their surviving work allows us to analyse royal sculpture over several decades and bears witness to the refinement of the late International Gothic style promoted by both Charles V and his son Charles VI at the beginning of his reign.

Musician, carved on a console♦ of the Tour du Village.

♦**Maître des œuvres:** *The person responsible for coordinating construction work, called architect after the very end of the Middle Ages.*

♦***Thurifer:*** *An incense-bearer.*

♦***Console:*** *An ornamental bracket projecting from a wall.*

by having a second, much larger, enceinte built, he was in possession of all necessary funds. This enceinte was built between the very end of 1372 (or early 1373) and 1379-1380, a remarkably short period. Its layout, spread out over more than a kilometre, is designed in such a way as to protect both the existing edifices (that is, the old Capetian manor and its outbuildings) and unbuilt areas where Charles V would later order various buildings to be erected.

By launching this new construction project, Charles V wished to dispose of a fortress but also of larger residential accommodation. At the same time, he had three elements erected which completed his project and thereby conferred full meaning to it: a huge bailey to the north of the castle, a palatine reliquary chapel and a pleasure manor on the banks of the Marne.

In 1380 the castle at Vincennes stood as one of the most vast in Europe, but Charles V's intentions lay elsewhere: he aspired to create a political capital there, materialising in stone an idea found elsewhere in contemporary Europe - at Westminster for the English monarchs, at Marienburg Castle in Poland for the Teutonic knights, at the palace at Avignon for the pope and above all, in the Holy Roman Empire, with the election of Prague as capital and the construction of the neighbouring castle of Karlstein to house the regalia or imperial emblems. In fact, Charles V's Vincennes was a direct consequence of the emergence of innovative forms for running the royal government. In a grandiose style, this immense castle expresses the birth of the modern State.

The castle bailey

The bailey was laid out between 1373 and 1385 on a square plan, its west and east sides prolonging the castle enceinte northwards up to what is now Rue du Midi. It was surrounded by a moat, probably reinforced by an embankment topped by a palisade or wall. As was usual in medieval fortified architecture, the bailey housed the domestic services of the Royal Household, in particular menservants and some of the provisions. There was also a rubbish dump and various installations including the lime kilns required for the never-ending work demanded by a castle of such scale. The bailey's size (nearly 4 hectares) says much about the need for space that the King's regular presence demanded: it meant that, around 1385, Vincennes was a fortified residence with a total surface area of about 9 hectares.

The interior of the castle, looking from the north southwards, from the Tour du Village. This mid-17th century engraving shows, in the left foreground, some vestiges of the medieval Capetian manor (private coll.).

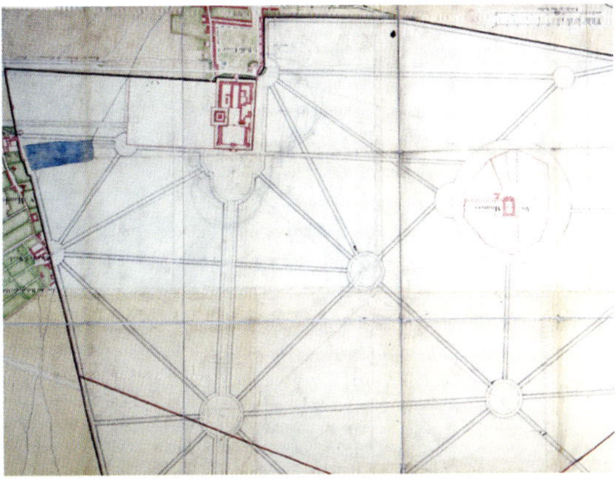

Plan of Vincennes forest in the 18th century. Since the 12th century the large circular enclosure, to the east of the castle and in the heart of the forest, had sheltered a priory of the Grandmont order (Vincennes, Service historique de la Défense, Minutes de la carte des chasses).

The Manor of Beauty as it remained in the early 17th century. Engraving by Claude Châtillon (Paris, BnF).

The Manor of Beauty

Charles V resided, worked and held audiences at Vincennes, the political capital, but he also wished to benefit from a personal and private "secondary" residence. In 1373 he therefore purchased land to the south-east of the forest, on the banks of the Marne, in order to have a park laid out. There, in 1376-1377, he had a house built called Manor of Beauty because of its charm and its attractive site. Entirely protected by an enceinte, this manor consisted of a square tower in which the king resided, a two-storey building and a chapel. A gravitation system conveyed spring water from Fontenay, to the north, to feed a fountain. The Manor of Beauty also had pleasure gardens, an orchard and a kitchen garden at its disposal. Charles V died there on 16 September 1380.

The palatine reliquary chapel

The founding of a reliquary chapel in November 1379, when the castle enceinte was practically finished, was a fundamental act by Charles V, who thereby concluded his architectural project.
Placed under the patronage of the Holy Trinity and the Blessed Virgin Mary, this foundation was ministered by a college of fifteen canons. Its canonical♦ status was based on that of the Sainte-Chapelle in Paris. As there, the main purpose of the Vincennes chapel was to appeal for heavenly protection over the royal residence and the dynasty by means of the perpetual celebration of divine office. Its creation was not a response to any architectural requirement. In addition to the chapels and oratories in the old Capetian manor, Charles V ordered a chapel dedicated to Saint Louis erected in

♦***Canonical:*** *According to or ordered by canon law which regulates the functioning of the Church.*

the keep enceinte and an oratory installed on the first, second and third storeys of the keep. Due to military and political conditions, work continued over a long period: began during Charles V's lifetime, it really only progressed in the 1390s during Charles VI's reign. Halted around 1405-1410 when the edifice was roofed but not vaulted, work was resumed briefly by François I before being completed by Henri II in 1552-1559.

The palatine reliquary chapel: cross-section of the nave, elevation of the west front, east-west cross-section, elevation of the south exterior (Paris, MAP).

From Charles VI to the late 16th century

The Château de Vincennes as it must have appeared circa 1400. In the foreground, on the left, the manor; beyond it, the palatine chapel under construction. Drawing by Jean-Claude Golvin.

Possessing a fortress like Vincennes at the very gates to Paris modified the living conditions of French royalty until around the mid-17th century. On several occasions when danger threatened, it was at Vincennes that the kings sought refuge: during Charles VI's reign (1380-1422), during the troubled times of Louis XI's reign (1461-1483), during the Wars of Religion and then during the minority of Louis XIII (1610-1643) and Louis XIV (1643-1715).

Under Charles VI, a disputed military base

Until 1397 Vincennes remained the habitual residence of Charles VI and his wife, Isabeau of Bavaria (1371-1435) following their marriage in 1385. Their first child was born there on 25 September 1386.
After the king's first attack of madness in 1392, his brother Louis d'Orléans gained in political importance, at the expense of his uncle Philip the Bold, Duke of Burgundy. The castle at Vincennes then became a coveted military base, especially when the conflict moved to an active phase after 1405 with the start of the quarrel between the Armagnac and Burgundian factions♦.
In 1420 Henry V, King of England, victor at the Battle of Agincourt in 1415, obtained the castle under the Treaty of Troyes. He installed himself there as his main residence and as an essential base for keeping a hold on the capital and the Île-de-France region. Having carried out repairs on the premises, he took many decisions at the castle where he died on 31 August 1422.
The Treaty of Arras signed on 20 September 1435 marked the reconciliation between the Duke of Burgundy and Charles VII (1422-1461), allowing the latter to reconquer the Île-de-France. The castle at Vincennes was taken on 19 February 1436. In spite of his triumphal entry into Paris in 1437, Charles VII stopped only very rarely in the capital or at Vincennes. Since his hasty departure in 1418 from Paris, seized by the Anglo-Burgundian faction, he had preferred the Berry and Loire valley regions.

A royal residence once more under Louis XI

Louis XI also privileged the Loire valley, but went fairly regularly to Vincennes, which he used as a base in 1465 at the time of the League of Common Weal♦.
In 1470 this monarch introduced a crucial break in the monumental history of the site: after having resided in the keep early in his reign, he commissioned a long pavilion erected in the south-west section of the castle enceinte. After the keep built in the 14th century one hundred metres to the south-west of the manor, the king's place of residence shifted for a second time.
His successors, Charles VIII (1483-1498), particularly during his youth, and Louis XII (1498-1515), frequented Vincennes, as did Anne de Bretagne (1477-1514), the wife successively of both monarchs.

♦**Armagnacs and Burgundians:** *During the Hundred Years War the Armagnacs were the Orleanist party, led by their count and supported by the nobility of the southern regions while the Burgundians derived support in the North and from the English.*

♦**League of Common Weal:** *An armed coalition of part of the aristocracy who waged war on Louis XII, led by Charles the Bold, Duke of Burgundy, in 1465.*

François I and Henri II: completion of the palatine reliquary chapel

Early in his reign, François I (1515-1547) went to Vincennes fairly often. In 1539, to welcome the Holy Roman Emperor Charles V (who in fact never came), he had the castle restored, in particular the building erected under Louis XI in the south-west sector of the enceinte. In 1520, to show gratitude for the fact that "it had pleased God to give him a fine son who could reign after him", he had given orders to "complete and perfect the fabric and edifice of the holy chapel". All that remained for Henri II (1547-1559) to do when work resumed around 1547-1548 was to have the vaulting constructed and execute the interior decor, in particular the panelling and stained glass. In 1552 the chapel, begun in 1379, was inaugurated by the king and his court.

Connétable de Montmorency and Henri II, also portrayed on the stained-glass windows of the chancel in the palatine chapel. Pen-and-ink and watercolour drawings, late 17th century (Paris, BnF, Clairambault).

A refuge during the Wars of Religion

By 1560 Catherine de' Medici (1519-1589) planned to create two pavilions to the south of the medieval enceinte. With France embroiled in the Wars of Religion, it again became a question of possessing a safe but equally fashionable residence very close Paris. During Charles IX's reign (1560-1574) the court sought refuge at Vincennes on several occasions. The king expired there on Whit Sunday 1574, two years after the Saint Bartholomew's Day Massacre. Under Henri III (1574-1589), Vincennes, the king's favourite residence, was also greatly coveted by the members of the Catholic League. Henri IV (1589-1610) entered Paris on 22 March 1594, taking possession of the castle on 28 March after the fortress had been evacuated by the League troops who had occupied it for several years. Henri IV visited often, but never stayed for very long.

Left
The palatine chapel, west front.

Final splendours of the 17th and 18th centuries

The pavilion of Marie de' Medici

After the assassination of her husband Henri IV, Marie de' Medici (1573-1642), anxious to protect herself and her young son, launched a vast programme of repairs and alterations to the castle. On 17 August 1610 she had the young Louis XIII (1610-1643), then aged nine, lay the cornerstone of an edifice destined to replace the Louis XI and François I pavilion. The latter, narrow and impractical, accommodated Louis XIII throughout his adolescence.

The classical palace

In 1652 the position of Governor of Vincennes passed to Cardinal Mazarin (1602-1661) who wished to have a well-protected residence at the gates of Paris, capable of sheltering what remained of his rich collections, plundered in 1651 during the Fronde♦. A new era opened for the castle.

♦**Fronde:** *Uprisings against the absolutism of the crown in France during the minority of Louis XIV.*

At the time Louis XIV (1643-1715) was looking for a new residence; Vincennes was favourably considered. In 1654 the architect Louis Le Vau drew plans for a large building (now called the King's Pavilion), completed in 1658. It encompassed Louis XIII's pavilion, doubling its width. The king sojourned frequently at Vincennes in those days, and it was probably at his prompting, more than that of Mazarin, that the project assumed its large scale.

A contract signed on 27 May 1658 provided for the construction of the Queen's Pavilion and of large outbuildings in the north half of the enceinte. A classical garden, with orangery, kiosks, ice house and other amenities was laid out to the west of the castle, while the wall surrounding the woods, whose surface was extended towards the south, was rebuilt. The castle's water system was completely overhauled. A wide road, ancestor of the present Avenue de Paris, was laid out

Hunting in the forest at Vincennes at the time of Louis XV, with the castle in the background. In this topograpical engraving, the image is reversed (Paris, musée Carnavalet).

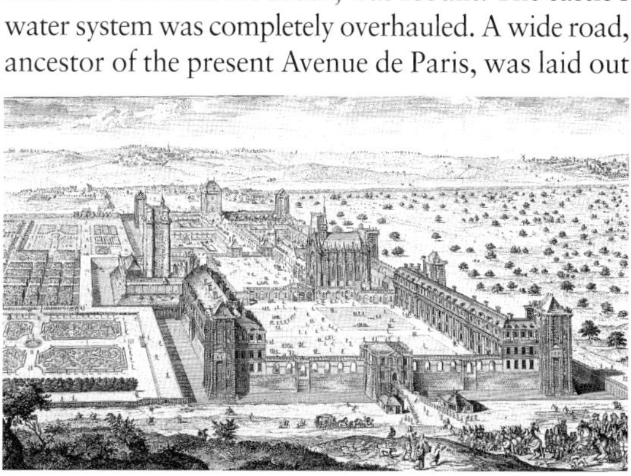

Perspective view of the castle in 1668, after completion of Louis XIV's work. Engraving by Pierre Brissart (Paris, musée du Louvre).

by Le Vau in 1660 between Place du Trône (now Place de la Nation) and the turret of Saint-Mandé which had marked the north-west corner of the woods' enclosure since the late 13th century. All this work was terminated in time to welcome the king and his wife after their wedding, celebrated at Saint-Jean-de-Luz. They arrived with the court at Vincennes on 19 June 1660 and remained there until their solemn entry into Paris on 26 August 1660.

The decorators hired by Le Vau – some of whom worked for Nicolas Fouquet at the Château de Vaux-le-Vicomte –

The Tour du Bois, transformed into a triumphal arch by Le Vau, served as the king's entrance. The sculptures installed on the terrace roof no longer exist (Paris, BnF).

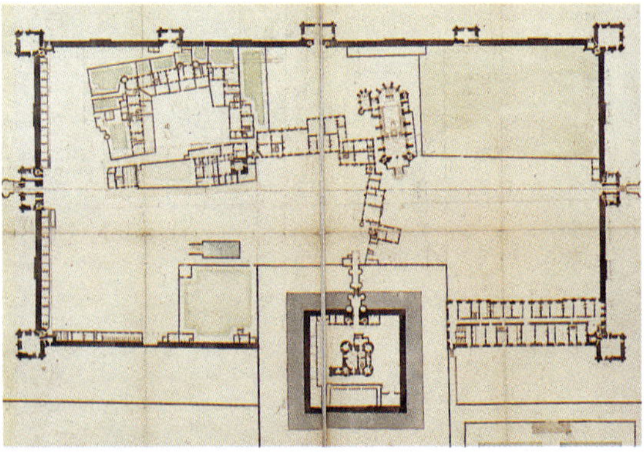

This document, executed by Le Vau in 1654, shows, in the upper left corner, the plan of what then remained of the Capetian manor (Bibliothèque historique de la Ville de Paris).

turned the King's and Queen's Pavilions into models of pre-Classical decoration, under Philippe de Champaigne's direction, assisted by his nephew Jean-Baptiste Champaigne, the Flemish artist Manchole, the Italian Borzone and the Frenchmen Baptiste Sève and Michel Dorigny (son-in-law of the painter Simon Vouet). The king himself indicated to the painters and sculptors the topics to be treated, such as the Treaty of the Pyrenees, signed in 1659, and his marriage with the Infanta Maria Theresa of Spain (1638-1683).

In addition to the two pavilions, Le Vau designed some immense outbuildings in the north half of the enceinte and, above all, installed a courtyard between the two pavilions. In order to do so, he opened up two sets of seven wide bays in the south medieval curtain wall♦ and transformed the Tour du Bois into a triumphal arch through which the monarch

♦***Curtain wall:*** *A segment of fortified wall between two towers.*

thereafter entered the castle. On the opposite side, and in order to enclose this courtyard to the north, Le Vau linked the two pavilions by a portico, demolished in 1837-1838 and rebuilt identically in 1967.
When the court was in residence, ceremonies and spectacles were organised at Vincennes. There in 1659 a French opera written and set to music by librettist Pierre Perrin (known as Abbé Perrin) and organist Robert Cambert was performed for the first time. *La Pastorale d'Issy* launched the genre that Jean-Baptiste Lully (1632-1687) was to make famous. Other spectacles followed during the summer of 1660.
Mazarin died at the castle on 9 March 1661. A mortuary chapel, installed in the choir of the reliquary chapel, held his mortal remains until their transfer in 1684 to the Collège des Quatre-Nations in Paris (now the Institut de France), founded with a bequest in his will.

Gradual abandonment of the castle

The court's installation at Versailles in 1682 meant the abandonment of Vincennes. On 9 September 1715, shortly after Louis XIV's death and in accordance with his explicit wish, the young Louis XV (1715-1774), his successor, was brought to Vincennes, followed by the court. However, by 30 December, the King moved to the Tuileries Palace in Paris before returning to Versailles. While later on occasion the king sojourned at Vincennes, in particular for hunting, the court never went back there.
Towards the end of the monarchy, the role bestowed on the castle was ill-defined. When Louis XV created the École Militaire in 1751, the company of non-commissioned officers and their pupils were housed

This illustration of a session of the Regency council in 1715 evokes the fleeting presence of the court shortly after Louis XIV's death and shows the dining-room décor in the King's Pavilion (château de Versailles).

Ewer and basin manufactured by the Vincennes porcelain factory in 1753-1754 (Paris, musée du Louvre).

in the King's Pavilion, abandoned in 1756 when the architect Jacques Ange Gabriel's military academy buildings at Grenelle were finished. At a time when industry was quasi-inexistent in Paris and its suburbs, the royal administration authorised pre-industrialisation experiments at Vincennes. A porcelain factory created in 1740 in the Tour du Diable was later enlarged and transformed into a royal factory before being transferred to Sèvres in 1756. There followed a weapons factory, then a faience and porcelain pottery "in the Strasbourg manner" (1767-1786).

From 1784 to 1790, after the keep was abandoned as a jail and prisoners transferred to the Bastille, an industrial bakery supplying the east of Paris was set up in the keep and its courtyard. Jean-Baptiste de Gribeauval (1715-1789), inspector of the royal artillery corps and renowned reformer, installed a weapons factory in the keep enceinte. At the start

Prince de Bourbon-Conti hunting near the Château de Vincennes. Oil on canvas by Jean-Baptiste Martin (1659-1735) (château de Versailles).

•Lettre de cachet: *An order under the king's private seal, for imprisonment or exile without a trial.*

Right-hand page, bottom **Mirabeau** on the keep terrace with, on the left, the Bastille, another symbol of oppression denounced in his essay *Des lettres de cachet et des prisons d'État,* published anonymously in 1782 (Vincennes, archives municipales).

of the Revolution, in spite of its excellent results, this enterprise using remarkably precocious standardised fabrication techniques was brought to a halt.

From 1777 to 1784 horse racing in the Vincennes forest led to increased frequentation of the district, but royalty finally deserted the scene. The castle was removed from the list of royal residences in 1784. In 1787 the king abolished the chapel's college of canons and put all the buildings up for sale. In 1788 their demolition was envisaged.

Prisoners in the keep

The courtyard installed as an exercise yard. The railings around the roof terrace were intended to prevent prisoners from committing suicide. Anonymous watercolour, circa 1808-1810 (Sceaux, musée de l'Île-de-France).

It was the duty of the monarch, as supreme judge, to make prisons available in his residences. We know that Louis XI housed certain eminent prisoners with him in the keep. During the 16th and 17th centuries, when the monarchs moved into the pavilion in the south-west sector of the castle enceinte, the keep was used solely as a prison. Henri de Navarre, the future Henri IV, was "accommodated" there in 1574. Henri II de Condé, imprisoned for his participation in the Fronde, spent three years there with his wife. Jean-François Paul de Gondi, Cardinal de Retz (1613-1679) remained a captive from 1652 to 1664 in the large second-storey chamber. Nicolas Fouquet (1615-1680), arrested in September 1661, was escorted to the keep while the king and his court were in residence.

The 18th century saw an increased use of *lettres de cachet*♦, signed by the king, transmitting orders of imprisonment in the keep on royal initiative or at the request of a family concerned, for example, with ridding itself of a troublesome son or helping him avoid more severe punishment. The *lettres de cachet* which caused the greatest repercussions concerned a category of prisoners unknown during earlier centuries: men of letters, such as Denis Diderot, incarcerated from July to October 1749. A dozen prisoners were held in the keep in 1754, thirty during troubled periods. Amongst the illustrious prisoners, names include Jean Henri Latude, incarcerated for thirty-five years in the Bastille or at Vincennes, notorious for his multiple escapes from both prisons, as well as the Marquis de Sade (1740-1814) detained in the keep from 13 February 1777 to 29 February 1784. Honoré de Mirabeau (1749-1791), condemned to death for abduction and seduction but reprieved from this sentence thanks to a *lettre de cachet* obtained by his family, was shut up in the keep for forty-two months, from 8 June 1777 to 22 October 1780. There he wrote numerous works including the essay *Des lettres de cachet et des prisons d'État* [*Of* Lettres de cachet *and of State Prisons*], published in 1782, which played an important role in public condemnation of this judicial system, in the development of the myth of the Bastille and Vincennes as symbols of oppression, and in the royal decision of 1784 to cease using the keep as a prison. The keep did however become a prison again in 1808 when Napoleon ordered the destruction of the Temple prison in Paris where Louis XVI and his family had been detained and which had become a Royalist pilgrimage site. The prisoners still there were transferred to Vincennes, at the same time as two objects, sole vestiges of the Temple prison and, for that reason, classified as historic monuments: an armoured door (deposited on the ground floor) and a white-tiled stove from Marie-Antoinette's cell (installed on the fifth floor of the keep).

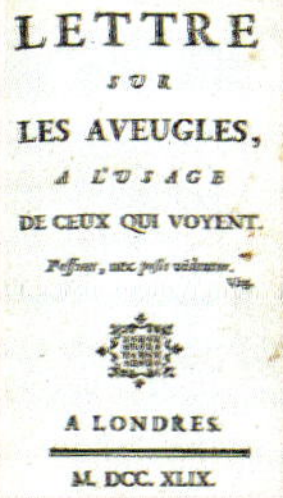
LETTRE
SUR
LES AVEUGLES,
A L'USAGE
DE CEUX QUI VOYENT.
Possunt, nec posse videntur. Virg.
A LONDRES.
M. DCC. XLIX.

The *Lettre sur les aveugles, à l'usage de ceux qui voyent* [*Essay on Blindness*], published anonymously by Diderot in 1749, led to his imprisonment (private coll.).

From barracks to public park: 19th-20th centuries

The Revolutionary period and the First Empire

The Revolutionaries decided to revert the keep to a prison, but the Parisians' opposition prevented the project from coming to fruition. In 1796 the Directory moved the Arsenal from Paris to Vincennes, its conversion thereby saving the monument. The Napoleonic wars, in particular the Russian Campaign, developed the Arsenal's activities, but not without destruction:

the enceinte towers, poorly maintained, were truncated between 1805 and 1820 (except for the Tour du Village which retained its full height, and the Tour du Bois already lopped off in the 17th century). The chapel, cut in half by a floor, was transformed into a warehouse, and the King's and Queen's Pavilions became barracks.

Maréchal de Mac-Mahon leaving the castle by the Tour du Bois to attend the great review held on the range, 15 September 1878. *Le Monde illustré*, 21 September 1878 (Vincennes, Bibliothèque du Service historique de la Défense).

An advanced fort defending Paris

During the Restoration (1815-1830) and under the July Monarchy (1830-1848) the buildings at Vincennes housed troops from the royal guard responsible for ensuring government safety. The role of artillery, in full development at the time, was crucial. In 1826 an artillery academy was founded there, disbanded only in 1944. To the south of the castle, deep in the forest, a range served as a drill ground, sometimes with unfortunate consequences for the inhabitants of towns to the south.

Having learnt the lesson from the allied troops' easy entry into Paris in 1814 and 1815, the Restoration and later July Monarchy governments (under Louis XVIII, Charles X and Louis-Philippe) wished to fortify the capital. Opinions diverged, however, between advocates of an unbroken wall and those opting for free-standing forts. As a result, until 1840 work was carried out only at Mont Valérien to the west and Vincennes to the east where casemates were erected between 1832 and 1843 against the medieval enceinte wall, most of which still exist. In 1840 tension in Europe led to the decision to construct a wall around Paris, preceded by forts. The castle transformation was terminated rapidly and between 1841 and 1844 the new fort built to the east. Thereafter it formed a single huge rectangular enclosure with the old medieval castle; the Tour des Salves served to communicate between what the military thereafter called the old fort (i.e. the castle) and the new fort. In 1931 the opening of what is now Cours des Maréchaux between those two architectural complexes freed the medieval building on that side to allow direct access between the town of Vincennes and the forest. During the Second Empire, Napoleon III maintained within the castle one of the largest garrisons of the Paris region. At the same

Général Daumesnil (Archives of the Société des amis de Vincennes).

Duc de Montpensier. Engraving after a painting by Winterhalter, 1844 (Archives of the Société des amis de Vincennes).

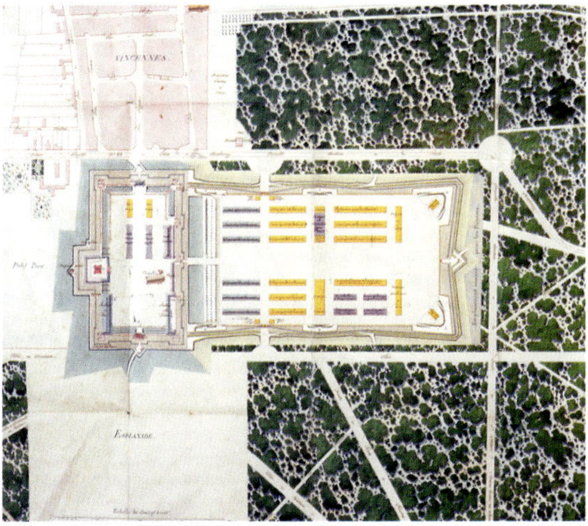

The castle and the new fort then under construction. This plan dating from 1842 shows the considerable area covered by this military complex (Vincennes, Service historique de la Défense, Archives du Génie).

time there was an evident increased military takeover of the forest, a very large portion becoming a drill ground. However Napoleon III wanted to create to the east of Paris an equivalent of the Bois de Boulogne, the latter recently transformed into a public park. Design work for the Bois de Vincennes began shortly before 1860. Except for the military installations, the park was transferred on 24 July 1860 to the City of Paris (which still owns it) and attached to the capital's 12th *arrondissement*.

The pupils of École polytechnique defending the eastern approaches to Paris against the allied troops in March 1814 (Archives of the Société des amis de Vincennes).

The explosion of the cartridge factory at Vincennes on 14 July 1871 (Vincennes, archives municipales).

The War of 1870♦ and the Commune♦

It was from the castle that the only real counter-offensive against the rapid advance of the Prussian troops was launched during the siege of the capital. The governor of Paris installed General Headquarters there, and the days of 27 and 28 November 1870 were used to gather troops in order to launch the offensive: on 30 November 1870 the French troops crossed back over the Marne river. After several days of fierce fighting, the army finally withdrew.

On 20 March 1871, two days after the beginning of the Paris uprising, the national guards arrived in front of the castle. The troops fraternised with the insurgents who took over the fort and refused to budge. On 27 May 1871 a colonel from the Versailles government came to negotiate their capitulation. On 28 May, after the executions at Père-Lachaise cemetery, only the castle at Vincennes still flew the red flag. The next day, when fighting abated in Paris, the proposed capitulation was accepted. Certain of the commanding officers of the garrison were shot in the south

♦***The War of 1870:*** *The Franco-Prussian war, a conflict which led to the downfall of Napoleon III.*

♦**The Commune:** *A revolutionary government in Paris, March-May 1871, ruthlessly suppressed.*

moat, a hundred metres west of the spot where the Duc d'Enghien had been executed in 1804, commemorated by a plaque at the base of the wall between the Tour du Roi and the Tour du Bois.

The Third Republic

After the 1870-1871 defeat, the government engaged in military reforms resulting, at Vincennes, in new constructions in the north section of the enceinte. The forest was provided with more amenities, both military and civil, including, in 1931, the "Colonial Exhibition" around Lake Daumesnil and, in 1934, the Vincennes zoo installation on 14 hectares.
Interest in the castle as an historic monument first appeared as early as 1793 with the removal and conservation of the stained-glass windows from the palatine reliquary chapel. In 1853 this chapel was classified as an historic monument and its restoration began in 1854 under the direction of Viollet-le-Duc. Classification of the keep followed in its turn in 1913 and its restoration launched after World War I. From then on numerous design and improvement projects were proposed, but they were brought to a halt by changes in international relations. In 1936 an underground complex was excavated under the casemates in the south-west corner of the enceinte, near the Queen's Pavilion, to serve as Chief-of-Staff Headquarters. From September 1939 to June 1940 this underground command post housed Generals Maurice Gamelin (1872-1958) and Maxime Weygand (1867-1965), successive Chiefs of Staff of the French army. The German army took possession of the castle on 14 June 1940 and used it, like the new fort, as barracks, prison and execution site. It was in the new fort that, on 23 December 1940, Jacques Bonsergent, the first Parisian, was shot having been arrested on 10 November after a street fight with German soldiers.
On 24 August 1944 the first units of the French 2nd Tank Division, under the command of General Leclerc, reached the Paris City Hall. That same evening the German troops fled the new fort and the castle after destroying three munitions depots. Their explosion led to the burning-down of the King's and Queen's Pavilions and opened a breach in the north-west curtain wall between the keep and the Tour de Paris. The following day General Leclerc and his division occupied the centre and west of the capital while the 4th US Infantry Division, under the command of General Barton, occupied the east of the capital and its eastern suburbs.

Left-hand page, bottom
The gathering of French troops
in the forest of Vincennes on 27 and 28 November 1870, prior to the counter-offensive on 30 November (Vincennes, archives municipales).

The King's Pavilion after the fire and explosion of a munitions depot during the night of 24-25 August 1944. Watercolour by Louis Bertin-Moreau (ERCVBE archives).

Towards the rehabilitation of the site

By late August 1944, Jean Trouvelot, architect-in-chief of Monuments historiques, had consolidated the damaged buildings. In 1947 a general restoration programme was drawn up, implemented by Jean Trouvelot. From 1953 to 1961 he restored the Queen's Pavilion and, from 1961 to 1978, the King's Pavilion. The portico closing off the courtyard to the north of the two classical pavilions, erected by Le Vau and demolished in 1837-1838, was rebuilt

The decoration of the Queen's guards' room or pages' room in the King's Pavilion, after its restoration by Jean Trouvelot (Paris, MAP).

identically in 1967, but the breach in the west curtain wall caused by the explosion of 24 August 1944 was not filled until 1990.

In 1948 the installation of the army's history department, followed a little later by those of the air force and navy, gave Vincennes a function corresponding to its historical interest and architectural qualities. In fact, due to the volume of archives, publications and maps kept there, it has become the third most important monument to national memory in France after the Archives nationales and the Bibliothèque nationale de France. In 1959 a project for transferring the official residence of the President of the Fifth Republic to Vincennes was evoked, but never realised.

Following the 1986 report by Jean-Philippe Lecat, a former minister, the Ministries of Culture and of Defence, to which the Vincennes site is allocated, united efforts to launch a vast pluriannual restoration, development and scientific study programme. The castle is thus gradually regaining an aspect worthy of the central role it played in French history from the late 12th century to the present.

Vincennes in 1946. On the left, the holy chapel, then the Queen's Pavilion. At this stage of the work, the casemates that concealed the south curtain wall and the Tour du Bois, to the right, were all demolished (Paris, MAP/AP).

Visit

The visit of Château de Vincennes begins in the ticket office-boutique housed in a 19th-century military building constructed at the edge of the paved central alley. Within the casemates of the keep, a scale model enables visitors to comprehend the overall site organization and a film presents the history and the restoration campaign of the keep. The palatine reliquary chapel, recently restored after serious damage caused by the storm of 1999, allows visitors to discover the wealth of its sculpted and painted decoration.

The medieval manor during excavations.
Below
Glazed ceramic tiles, from one of the floors dating from Charles V's reign, discovered on this occasion.

The manor

The manor, known through written sources, a few pre-1650 depictions and, above all, the archaeological excavations carried out between 1992 and 1996, was composed of a series of buildings erected gradually from the late 12th century.
In the 14th century they formed an irregular quadrilateral, each side about sixty metres. At the corner of the south and west wings stood a square keep; the chapel, dedicated to Saint Martin, was probably situated in the south wing and the great hall in the west wing.

The north and east sides of the manor were closed by a relatively thin wall pierced, to the east, by an entry framed by two turrets. Nonetheless the manor could not be considered a true fortified building: it was erected at ground level, not raised on a mound, and its surrounding wall, scarcely over a metre thick to the north, was not protected by a ditch. Recent excavations have revealed two levels of 13th- and 14th-century cellars, and a 13th-century fountain in the centre of the court, but renovated under Charles V. It remains the only surviving evidence of the manor.

Statues of Charles V and his wife, Jeanne de Bourbon, stood in two of the three central niches. Higher up, a console bore a depiction of the Holy Trinity.

The keep

The gatehouse

In the Middle Ages two doors served as entry into the keep enceinte. To the west, a small door opened on to gardens laid out on the exterior of the castle. This door, walled up at the beginning of Louis XIII's reign and recently uncovered, is visible from outside the castle. The main entry was situated to the east, towards the manor. A bridge serving two drawbridges provided access, one for pedestrians (since disappeared) and one for carriages (reinstalled). The gatehouse, consisting of two towers framing the entry, is crowned by a terrace. Its tall vault was closed by a door preceded by a portcullis (the trace of which can still be seen in the architecture) and by *assommoirs*, vertical or oblique slots from which missiles were hurled on attackers. Charles V's study (greatly restored before World War II) was located above this entrance vault: a square room, heated by a fireplace, flanked in each of the two towers by a room (also heated by a fireplace) wherein the king's notary secretaries, his permanent collaborators, were installed. The gatehouse's east façade bore a carved decoration where now only traces remain. Five niches held five statues: in the centre, Saint Christopher flanked by the royal couple. Between these three central recesses and the two lateral ones, a shield bearing the arms of France surmounting another shield presenting a dolphin (all hacked and defaced in 1793) recalled that Charles V, patron of the building, had been the first Dauphin of France in 1349. Higher up, according to a text dating from 1378, above the king's study window, a console bore a statue of the Holy Trinity, invoking divine protection for the monarch. Charles V's study is reached by a staircase of major proportions (3.32m diameter), accessible from the keep courtyard. It presents some exceptional features, analogous to those Raymond du Temple, Charles V's chief architect, executed at the Louvre Palace during exactly the same period. The staircase partially projects beyond the main construction, with four superposed bays opened widely onto the exterior.

Charles V holding a model of a church and his sceptre (Paris, musée du Louvre).

The west façade of the gatehouse and the footbridge leading to the first storey of the keep, reinstalled in 1934 in the same place as the original entrance. This bridge was the only means of access to the keep during the Middle Ages.

Charles V and mechanical clocks

Elevation of the east side of the keep and gatehouse in 1814.
The medieval bell was still in place above a clock face dating from 1768 which can now be seen on the north side of the Tour du Village. Watercolour drawing by warrant officer Benard (Paris, MAP).

By 1369 the Vincennes bell tower crowning the gatehouse terrace was equipped with a clock, probably made by Henri de Vic, a native of the Meuse-Rhine region. Charles V took great interest in mechanical clocks which were becoming widespread throughout contemporary Europe. This innovation was then highly expensive because its mechanism had to be constantly rewound and the hands adjusted, necessitating a salaried and resident keeper. In order to strike the hours, the clock was fitted with a bell weighing a total of 714.41 kg. An inscription on this bell records that it was cast, on Charles V's behest, by Jean Jouvente who worked simultaneously for other royal residences, in particular for the Palais de la Cité, Paris, in 1370-1371. The position of this clock at Vincennes, above the king's study, opposite and on the same level as his bedchamber in the keep, is noteworthy. After this one, Charles V had clocks installed in all his important Parisian residences, each time for religious reasons: to organise his life, in every season, in accordance with the canonical hours, that is, according to the times of day which, in the Catholic liturgy, correspond to the recitation of certain parts of the breviary.

The Vincennes bell, a rare and handsome object, bears witness to the psychology of a medieval monarch. Commissioned by the king for one of the earliest monumental clocks in France, this bell is the oldest one surviving in Île-de-France, after that of the church of Saint-Merri in the capital. It is now presented in the palatine chapel. The bell tower, partially razed in the 19th century and restored in 2000, has been fitted with a replica.

The bell from the gatehouse clock, cast in 1369.

The keep, a remarkable construction

The king's bedchamber on the second storey.

The capital of the central column, before restoration in 1930, bearing a painted decoration. Watercolour by Louis Bertin-Moreau (ERCVBE archives).

With the destruction of the keep at Coucy in 1914, the Vincennes keep became the tallest in Europe. It is also a monument of very great daring, with its height of 50 metres and its vaults on every storey (except one). Its overall equilibrium posed formidable problems for Raymond du Temple who implemented innovative techniques and architectural solutions for this exceptional edifice, simultaneously a royal residence and the symbol of strength and authority.

This square tower, each side measuring 16.5 metres, is flanked at each corner by a salient circular turret with a 6.6-metre diameter. Pinned to the north of the north-west turret, a projecting rectangular tower with flat buttresses (5m by 6m) contains latrines which served the first five storeys. The walls of the central body of the keep are so thick (3.26 metres!) that, within, the architect was able to install corridors, a staircase and oratories.

Each of the keep's eight storeys holds a square central room with sides measuring almost 10 metres. On the first four levels, the central column is decorated with a fine sculpted capital completed on the periphery by eight consoles. The height under the keystone is 7 metres on the ground floor and 8 metres on the first, second and third storeys.

Under the floor of the third and fourth storeys, arches spring from the corners and middle of the central room walls to relieve the central column of some of its load. This relief system is reinforced by an extraordinary utilisation of iron: over one and a half kilometres of iron bars in various forms (each with a section of several centimetres) were integrated into the building structure during construction. The door and window lintels, like the slabs covering the corridors cut into the wall thickness, are supported by bars of this type. More exceptionally, it has been discovered that the entire exterior of the keep has been encircled by hooping at the floor level of the fourth and fifth storeys. Finally, horizontal metal tie-beams were disposed about 10 centimetres under the floor along the median lines of the central rooms on the third, fourth and fifth storeys.

Diagonal and median sections of the keep and buttress arcs of the central column under the floor of the third and fourth storeys. Drawings by Agence Dominique Moufle, ACMH.

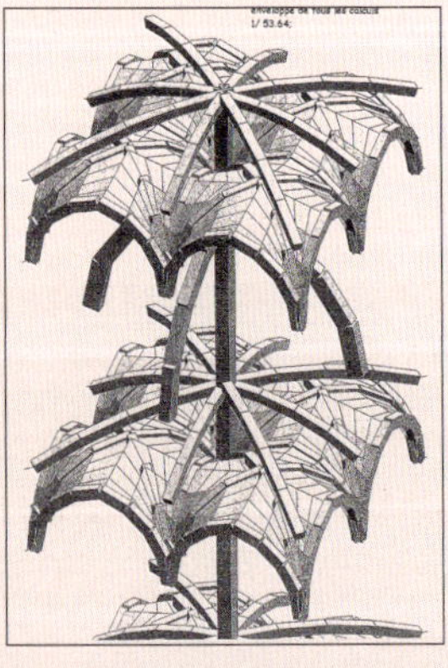

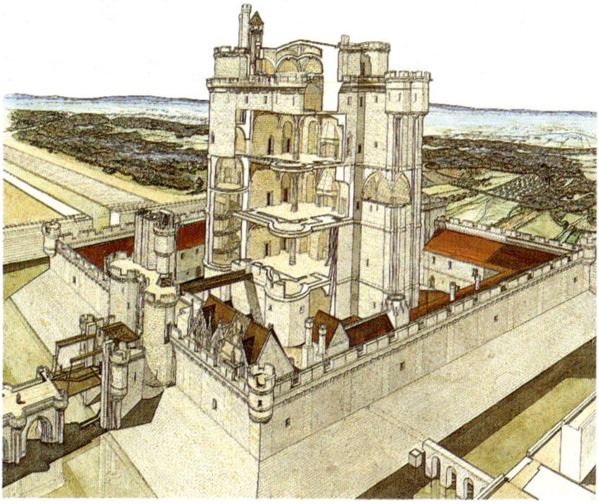

The keep and its enceinte at the time of Charles V. The king had two apartments: one at the level of the parapet walk of the keep enceinte, the other, his "upper chamber", on the second storey of the keep. Watercolour drawing by Jean-Claude Golvin.

An eight-sided vault (destroyed in 1840 and rebuilt in 2000) covered this staircase which gives access to the gatehouse terrace.

The enceinte

The construction method of the defence wall contrasts with that of the gatehouse and keep. This irregular square with sides each measuring a little over 50 metres in length and high, thick walls (11.5 metres by 1.7 metres) consists of stone bond toothing♦ which frame rubble-masonry panels. Three levels of superposed consoles, with machicolations♦ of the same width pierced between them, form its crown. This defensive system, innovative at the time, would become common by the late 14th century. The four watchtowers set at the corners of the enceinte and the parapet walk served originally as an ambulatory. At first the parapet walk was open, then during the 15th century roofed with tiles and finally, early in Louis XIII's reign, with slate (as seen now) with pointed roofs for the watchtowers instead of the original crenellated terraces. Above the parapet walk level and in the north-east corner of the enceinte were buildings of which some vestiges of rooms remain, recognised through early documents. Situated on the same level as the king's second-floor study in the gatehouse, these rooms (a chapel dedicated to Saint Louis, a hall and a bedchamber), together with his study, constituted the king's lower apartments.

Circulation

In the Middle Ages the only access to the keep was through its first floor (the two ground-floor doors were pierced in the 18th century), by means of a footbridge which, like today, led from the terrace in front of the king's gatehouse study. Cut into the thickness of the south wall, a small spiral staircase (mainly reserved for servants) served all the storeys of the keep, from the ground floor to the terrace. The great staircase, reserved on the contrary for the king to move between the two noble storeys – the first and second floors – was installed when the second floor of the keep had already been built.

♦Toothing: *Here bonded stones disposed vertically over the whole height of a wall and limiting panels constructed of rubble masonry.*

♦Machicolation: *An opening installed in the floor of projecting sections of a building allowing defenders to fire downwards or to drop various missiles on attackers.*

Painted decor of the enceinte parapet walk (16th century), reconstituted in 1925. Watercolour by Louis Bertin-Moreau (ERCVBE archives).

The first floor

The great hall could serve as a council chamber or, if required, as a chamber for the king's close relations, such as the queen. The walls and vaulting of this hall were covered with oak panelling (still in place under the vaults), as was the small oratory installed in the north wall. A dendrochronological♦ study has shown that this panelling had been prepared from oaks felled between 1367 and 1371 in present-day Latvia or in Poland.

The second floor

The king's bedchamber has retained important traces of its decoration, dating from shortly after Charles V's installation in 1367-1368: the rib vaulting bears fleurs-de-lys modelled in relief, gilded with gold leaf, set against a blue background. Hooks still in place in the vaults and wall marks prove that the king's bedchamber was entirely panelled, like the oratory in the north wall and the south-west turret. The latrine walls and those of the "study" projecting out to the west of the latrine tower were also panelled.

The ground floor with the well and, on the right, the wall dividing the room in two.

The ground floor

This level contains a well and a large chimneypiece, the hood of which has since disappeared. Greatly altered in the 18th century when the keep served as a prison (the two doors opening on to the courtyard were cut through at that time), the ground floor probably originally served as a storage room and accommodation for friends and relations or servants rather than as a kitchen.

The central hall on the first floor of the keep, with the Baltic wood panelling set into the vaulting, its whitewash having been restored in 2006.

Baltic wood panelling installed at the top of the walls of the second-floor north-west turret. In contrast to those on the first floor, these wood panels were left untreated, without

Two carved consoles and two carved, painted bosses in the keep.

Charles V's bedchamber vault. The panelling has been removed but the painted decoration on the ribs, consisting of the king's arms of gilt fleurs-de-lys on a blue background, is still in place.

♦*Dendro-chronology:* *A method of dating based on analysing the annual growth rings of trees.*

Oratory vaults installed in the thickness of the north wall on the second storey of the keep. Like its equivalent on the first floor, this oratory was completely panelled. All that remains of this decoration are the battens on which the planks, now completely disappeared, were nailed.

The inventory of the royal collections drawn up in 1380 provides valuable information regarding the furniture, the many gems and the manuscripts kept in the king's bedchamber and its dependencies, all heated by fine hooded chimneypieces. A chest set in the west window recess held thirty-one religious manuscripts, including two psalters which had belonged to Saint Louis. The south-west turret held chests containing the king's linen. The north-west turret was the "retreat" where, from July 1367, the king's "coffers", that is, very large sums of money, were deposited. From there, the latrine tower is reached. A wood partition (since disappeared) separated the latrines strictly speaking from a vestibule where one of the doors leads, westwards, to the "study" where Charles V worked, surrounded by exceptional illuminated manuscripts, gems and relics. This small well-lit room, moreover, could be heated more easily that the great hall in the centre of the keep. The boss of its vaulting is decorated with a Holy Trinity; the ribs spring from four consoles carved with the symbols of the Evangelists. This sculpture dates from a little later that those in the rest of the keep, since the "study" was added a few years after completion of the second floor, although the fourth storey had already been built. The north-east turret, like its first- and third-floor equivalents, served as a chapel for celebrating the offices which were followed from the oratories installed on each of the three floors within the thickness of the north wall. This function explains why this turret is the only one to be provided with chimneypieces on each floor, unlike the other corner turrets of the keep's central body.

Psalter of Saint Louis. During Charles V's reign, this very luxurious manuscript, executed in Paris between 1255 and 1270, was kept in the bedchamber on the second storey of the keep (Paris, BnF).

Vincennes, an important royal building site

Charles V reading in his study. This illustration adorning a manuscript from Charles V's library could depict either the Louvre or Vincennes (Paris, BnF).

Stone supplied to the site came mainly from the quarries at Charenton and Conflans, to the south of the forest at the foot of the plateau overlooking the Marne and, to a lesser degree, from those at Gentilly and Ivry-Vitry, on the left bank of the Seine at the very gates of Paris. The stones forming the outer facing of the keep and its gatehouse and, above all, the castle enceinte are assembled particularly carefully with fine pointing.

Since the building accounts have not survived, the exact number of labourers employed on the site is unknown. We do however know that in 1363 there were eighty stone cutters, two hundred master masons and as many journeymen, one hundred varlets or attendants, and three hundred carts busy transporting the stone. A few estimates give an idea of the scale of the project. Between 1373 and 1380 excavation of the moat around the castle enceinte produced 350 000 cubic metres of waste. At the same time, some 260 000 limestone blocks, on average 32 centimetres high, 80 centimetres wide and 90 centimetres deep, were used merely for the outside facing of the curtain walls and towers, the counterscarp♦ wall and part of the inside facing of the enceinte. This called for the delivery, on average, of 130 blocks per working day, to which must be added the materials required for the internal rubble fill of the walls and the inside facing, together with specific items such as the stone for the doors, windows, loopholes♦ and buttresses, as well as all the carved elements. Such a project could not have been carried out, in just eight years, without very rigorous organisation. The numerous lapidary marks – more than six hundred different traces have been recorded on the castle enceinte stones – are marks used in the management of the stock of stones.

The rare surviving documents allow us to calculate that, between 1361 and 1380, work on the keep and the castle enceinte cost the king a total of several hundred thousand *livres*. This enormous sum covers not only the construction but also the expenses related to the enlargement of the forest, carried out at the same time by Charles V, as well as the interior fitting-out of the buildings. The cost of the latter, in such luxurious edifices as Vincennes and the Manor of Beauty, which the same king built in the forest from 1376 to 1377, must have been extremely high.

♦***Counterscarp:*** *The outer wall or slope of a ditch in a fortification.*

♦***Loophole:*** *A narrow vertical opening in a wall allowing arrows to be shot from a bow.*

The third floor

This level differs from the second only by the absence of the projecting "study", the painted decoration and the panelling. As, according to the 1380 inventory, this floor housed neither manuscripts nor jewels, this fact suggests that it was neither

Capital of the central column in the third-storey hall.

the queen's bedchamber nor the dauphin's but rather that of some other of the king's relations.

The three upper floors

These levels were intended for family or close relations and servants as well as domestic and military supplies, in particular for the engines of war installed in the fourth-floor windows and on the latrine tower terraces and the central body of the keep. On the fourth storey, four large arches springing from the centre of the walls and a central pillar carry a floor. On the fifth storey, the central pillar supports the springers of four vaults, with a height of only 3.5 metres under the keystone. A blind sixth storey, a mere 2-metres high in its tallest section, is accessible only through an opening cut in the centre of the summit terrace. Work was carried out in the keep when it was used as a prison in the 17th and especially 18th century. From 1752 in particular, an important campaign was undertaken: the bars at the windows and the many cell doors date from that period. Most of the 17th- and 18th-century graffiti and paintings are the work of prisoners. Some represent complex iconographic cycles, others are merely small decorative pictures or short inscriptions.

The keep seen from the south-east.

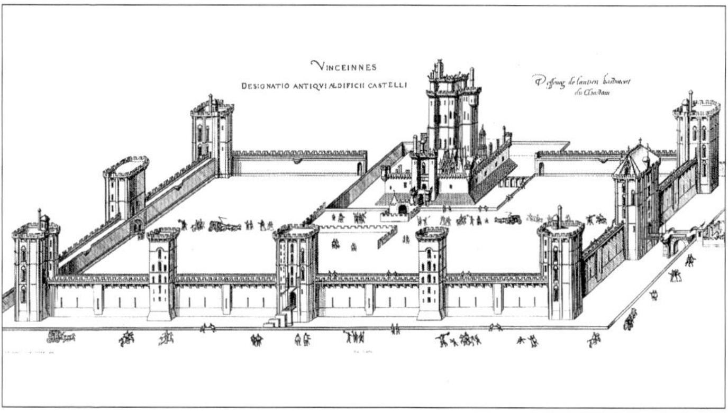

The castle enceinte

This new project, initiated late 1372 or early 1373, has the dimensions of an urban precinct, measuring over a kilometre in length. It was however carried out in record time, since all construction work was completed in 1379-1380. This enceinte is formed by two rectangles: the exterior counterscarp wall (389m by 226m) surrounding the interior enceinte wall (330m by approximately 180m). Between the counterscarp and the enceinte, the moats (25.5m wide to the west and east, 29.5m wide to the north and south) received, until the 19th century, the overflow of springs tapped from the Montreuil hills and of rain and waste waters from the various buildings protected by the enceinte, collected by a sewer system.
The curtain walls (2.6m thick) rise some 10 metres above the ground level court and 18 metres from the bottom of the moat which a general filling-in during the late 19th century raised 4.5 metres above its initial depth.
Nine towers defended the ten sections of the curtain walls. Rising originally about 40 metres over the bottom of the moat, they represent four different types: the Tour du Village, largest of all, is almost as big as the keep; the Tour des Salves and Tour du Bois serve, like the former, as entry gates; four towers form the corners; finally, the two smaller towers of the east curtain wall are the only ones without buttresses. Each of these towers had been designed more as a keep than as a simple wall tower. Their quadrangular plan and strong commanding position over the curtain wall make them exceptional in 14th-century fortified architecture, whether related to castle or city walls.
In fact, like the keep, they represented luxurious residential accommodation, attested by the quality and importance of the carved decoration on the exterior façades and the interior of the three entrance towers, and proved further by the number and size of the chimneypieces and windows, the dimensions of the spiral staircases and the existence of latrines on each storey.
In all, these towers represented a residential area of twenty-eight to thirty-three "chambers", representing 3 000 to 3 500 square metres of habitable space.
This residential function of the towers does not prevent the enceinte from having a definite military aspect: the considerable width and depth of the moat, like the height of the curtain walls, set the castle enceinte well above contemporary urban fortifications.

Perspective view of the castle circa 1575, *Les Plus Excellents Bâtiments de France*, by Jacques Androuet Du Cerceau, 1575-1579.
The great interest of this document is that it shows the enceinte towers with their original elevation. However the buildings occupying the interior of the enceinte, including the palatine chapel, are not depicted.

Defensive aspects were taken into consideration by ensuring the possibility of uninterrupted circulation on the parapet walk. The four superposed levels of loopholes or firing platforms installed in the enceinte (in the tower basements within the curtain walls at courtyard level, at the curtain wall summits and at the tower tops) provided good defensive possibilities. All these towers, except the Tour du Village, have been truncated: the Tour du Bois when it was transformed into a triumphal arch during Louis XIV's reign, the other seven between 1805 and 1820.
Occupied by various administrative departments, they are not open to the public.

Left-hand page
The Tour du Village
and its two pedestrian and cart drawbridges, reconstructed during the restoration work.

Exterior elevations and sections,
in 1818, of three enceinte towers before they were razed: Tour du Réservoir, Tour de la Surintendance and Tour des Salves. The first held, in its lower section, a large lead reservoir which supplied water to the castle. The Tour de la Surintendance and Tour du Diable were the only ones on the enceinte without buttresses. The Tour des Salves served as the east entrance; for this reason, like the other two entrances, Tour du Village and Tour du Bois, it had a highly decorated façade (Service historique de la Défense, archives du Génie).

The palatine chapel seen from the south-west.

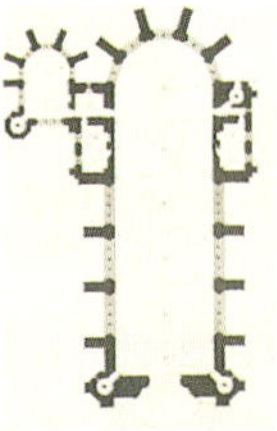

The palatine reliquary chapel

The chapel at Vincennes is modelled after Louis IX's Sainte-Chapelle in the Palais de la Cité, with a single difference: as two-storey edifices had gone out of fashion, the Vincennes chapel has only one storey. Its general elevation is very simple: tall windows, separated by deep buttresses and topped with gabled canopies, rise above a fairly sober base. A spire, pulled down in the late 18th century, rose above the fourth bay of the nave. Most of the external decoration dates from the period 1390-1410, as does the interior sculpted decoration. The window tracery, moving from Rayonnant Gothic in the choir to Flamboyant style in the nave, bears witness to the advancement of the construction from its start at the chevet♦. The west front, built last, well into the 15th century, is a fine example of Flamboyant architecture: the superposition of three ornate gabled pediments,

♦***Chevet:** The east end of a church, consisting of apse and ambulatory, semicircular, polygonal or even rectangular in plan (with or without radiating chapels); the term chevet is here reserved for the exterior wall.*

Depiction of the Holy Trinity, central keystone of the arch moulding on the west door.

each set back in relationship to the next, corresponds to a desire to set off the rose window.
The west portal is now deprived of all sculpture, apart from the recessed arch moulding over the door. Its central pier♦, which was adorned with a Virgin and Child, as well as the tympanum (its iconography unknown) were destroyed at the end of the 18th century.
Despite this defacement, experts consider that what remains of the west portal numbers among the finest surviving examples of early 15th-century sculpture, in particular the two seated prophets seen at the base, on the left and right, of the first voussoir♦.
At the very top of the arching, an arch-stone bears a figure of the Holy Trinity, to whom the chapel is dedicated. Unfortunately the names of the sculptors are unknown.
Apart from the west portal and the tympana, and the interior bosses

♦***Pier:*** *The solid masonry separating the two halves of a portal and bearing a tympanum or lintel.*

♦***Voussoir:*** *Each of the wedge-shaped or tapered stones forming an arch.*

and the consoles, the rest of the sculpted decoration dates from the 16th century. It is concentrated above the circulation gallery crowning the eaves walls♦. Visitors should note a salamander, emblem of François I (1515-1547) who had work resumed on the chapel. (One of these salamanders, removed during restoration work on the chapel in the early 1990s and replaced by a copy, is presented to the public in the chapel nave.)

*♦**Eaves wall:** A wall carrying a gutter or pipe made of metal or lead-covered wood placed under the overhang of a sloped roof in order to catch and direct rainwater through the downspouts or in the gargoyles.*

The interior

The chapel consists of a single nave with five bays, ending in a five-sided apse. The king's and queen's oratories flank the bay preceding the choir. To the north of the king's oratory, the sacristy is surmounted by a treasure room (closed to visitors). The tall windows rise above the plain base interrupted by a plant-decorated frieze punctuated by consoles. The interior decor is above all shaped by these strongly projecting and extremely elaborate consoles, and by the keystones of the sections already vaulted in the Middle Ages. Some of these keystones, in the two north and south oratories and along their access corridors, bear the arms of Isabeau of Bavaria who married Charles VI in 1385. This vaulting is thus posterior to that date. The arms of Jeanne de Bourbon, Charles V's wife, on the tympanum of the north oratory access corridor, and those of Isabeau of Bavaria, in the same location at the south corridor entrance, are early 19th-century restorations. The tympanum over the north sacristy door, on the other hand, is original. The meaning of the presence of prophets and other figures

Vaults with a painted decoration evoking, by the letters "H" and "K", Henri II and his wife Catherine de' Medici.

The Coronation of the Blessed Virgin, tympanum at the sacristy entrance.

The choir and its stained-glass windows dating from the 16th century.

Right-hand page **Stalls** set in place under Henri II and destroyed in 1793, like the rest of the interior decoration. Plate, A.-L. Millin, *Antiquités nationales*, Paris, 1790-1798.

The rose window in the west front seen from the tribune.

on the nave consoles is difficult to explain in the absence of the free-standing sculptures which must have occupied the niches above them.
The general iconography probably illustrated the classical parallel between the Old and New Testaments, doubtless beginning with the west portal decoration.
Under Henri II (1547-1559), Philibert Delorme oversaw construction work to finish the chapel and called on the French and Italian artists who were working under his direction at the Château de Fontainebleau.
The important interior decoration set in place at that time was largely destroyed in 1793. From 1551, meetings of the Order of Saint Michael (founded by Louis XI in 1469) were held in the choir, then enclosed by a wooden partition and fitted with eighty stalls for the knights of the order – of which the king was the grand master – executed by a famous sculptor of Italian origin, Francisque Scibec de Capri.
The vault decoration, with the initials "H" and "K" for the names of Henri II and Catherine de' Medici, was painted by Charles Carmoy, partially responsible for the decoration of the great gallery at Fontainebleau.

According to late 17th-century drawings, the crescent moons which alternate with the "H"s and "K"s in this painted decoration also appeared on the nave's stained-glass windows. The moon symbol refers to Henri II's two successive mottos: *Cum plena est, emula solis* (When it [the moon] is full, it is equal to the sun); *Donec totum impleat orbem* (Until it fills the whole circle). The reference is however not lacking in ambiguity, since it is also a discreet allusion to the king's mistress, Diane de Poitiers, as the mythological Diana

Stained glass in two of the apse windows, illustrating the Revelation to Saint John, restored twice during the 19th century, then again in the 20th century. The glass is for the most part original. In the bottom left section of the right-hand window the kneeling figure of Henri II wearing the ribbon of the Order of Saint Michael is a 19th-century copy.

was traditionally represented as a moon goddess.
In 1551, to complete the interior decoration, Philibert Delorme commissioned the stained glass for the chapel from Nicolas Beaurain, a glass painter who worked for various Parisian churches and for the royal chateaux of Fontainebleau and Saint-Germain-en-Laye, among others.
The Vincennes glass was installed between 1556 and 1559. The nave windows, already destroyed to a large degree by the end of the *Ancien Régime*, are known only through drawings; they bore a royal emblem on a white background, allowing light to flood the nave and the congregation to follow the office in their missals. By contrast, most of the choir stained glass has been preserved: the highly coloured windows recount the Apocalypse seen by Saint John the Apostle. They were restored twice in the 19th century, the first time occasioned by the transfer of the Duc d'Enghien's body to the chapel on Louis XVIII's orders.

Late 17th-century drawing showing the decoration of the nave stained-glass windows, completely destroyed at the end of the *Ancien Régime*. The motifs include their date of creation, MDLXXV, and the king's motto, *Donec totum impleat orbem* (Until it fills the whole circle), a reference to the moon, a royal symbol also found in the painted decoration of the chapel vaults (Paris, BnF).

The funerary monument in memory of the Duc d'Enghien

The execution of the Duc d'Enghien, engraving after a painting by Jean-Paul Laurens (Archives of the Société des amis de Vincennes).

The moat at Vincennes after the execution of the Duc d'Enghien (Archives of the Société des amis de Vincennes).

On 20 March 1804, in reprisal for a Royalist assassination attempt against Napoleon, the Duc d'Enghien was executed by firing squad in the castle moat near the Tour de la Reine, and buried on the same spot.

In 1816 Louis XVIII had the Duke's remains moved to the palatine chapel. A commemorative monument was erected and the building again used for worship. Following three successive proposals by the sculptor Louis-André Deseine, the monument was finally completed in 1825, three years after the sculptor's death.

Originally the monument was installed against the chapel's chevet wall. In April 1852 Louis Napoléon Bonaparte, hoping to have the scandal of the Duke's execution forgotten, had it removed from the chapel. Faced with protests, he had it set up in the north oratory, where it has remained.

To accommodate this transfer, the funerary monument base had been reconstructed in its present location in the oratory. It is surmounted by its four original statues, representing France and Crime (each 2.2 metres high) and, above, the Church and the Duke (each 2.5 metres high).

A Latin inscription evoking the Duc d'Enghien's death, engraved on a marble plaque, has been placed in front of his funerary monument.

The Tour du Roi, still with its original height, and the monument raised on the spot of the Duke's execution. Painting by François-Alexandre Perrot, 1822 (Angers, musée des Beaux-Arts).

The commemorative column.

Decor of the King's Pavilion, removed by Fontaine in order to be transported into the royal museum installed in the Louvre under Louis-Philippe. These rooms are now occupied by the Department of Egyptian Antiquities.

The King's Pavilion.

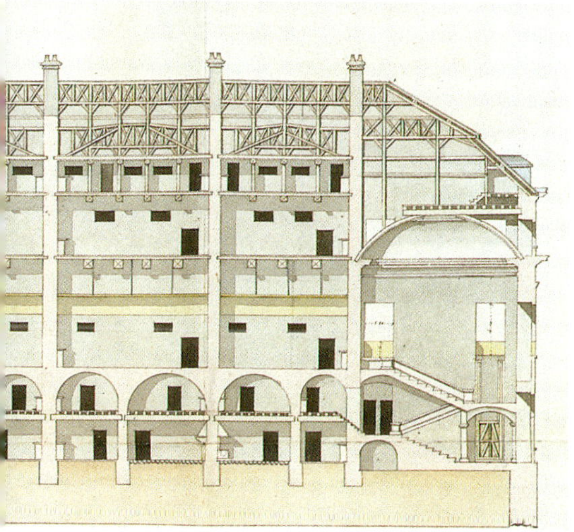

The King's Pavilion and Tower in the early 19th century. The tower had not yet been razed, and the internal structure of the pavilion was as originally designed. The great staircase, to the north of the building, was moved to the centre at the time of restoration work (Service historique de la Défense, atlas des bâtiments militaires).

The classical palace (1610-1617, 1654-1661)

Within the castle enceinte, all that remains of the south-west corner pavilion built at the beginning of Louis XIII's reign are the west façade, visible from the castle exterior, and the overall architectural structure. Between 1654 and 1658 Le Vau merged it into the present King's Pavilion, slightly longer in the north-south direction and twice as wide along the west-east axis. The Queen's Pavilion was build from 1658 to 1660, opposite and symmetrical to the King's Pavilion.

The interior arrangement and decor of the King's and Queen's Pavilion

In the King's Pavilion, on the first floor and on the side of the small park (that is, looking westwards towards the gardens), were five rooms forming the king's apartments. The queen's apartments over-looked the royal court, on the east side, while those of the dauphin and dauphine were on the north. Greatly damaged during the 18th and 19th centuries, the interior decoration of the two pavilions was almost completely destroyed by the fire of 24 August 1944. Restoration has totally modified the interior arrangements

The Queen's Pavilion, painted ceiling by Michel Dorigny.

of the King's Pavilion, where only a few vestiges of the painted decoration have survived (an arch in the ceiling and a few window recesses), whereas the Queen's Pavilion contains two restored ceilings with additions made in 1842 when Louis-Philippe's son, the fort commander, resided in this pavilion. Nonetheless, the decoration of the King's and Queen's Pavilions is known through the project drawings by Dorigny, one of the artists of Louis XIV's era, through early descriptions and through a few photographs taken prior to the 1944 fire.
Some panelling and painted ceilings from these pavilions, moved in the 19th century at the time the Musée du Louvre was being reorganised, can now be admired in its Department of Egyptian Antiquities.

The orangery, the 18th century

During the 18th century the castle buildings were occupied without any particular work being carried out, not even maintenance. The orangery, built up against the medieval wall to the east of the chapel chevet, is thus the only architectural testimony remaining from this period.
The orangery houses archives, inaccessible to the public.

The fortifications, the 19th century

Nothing remains from the First Empire except the installations erected to defend Paris against the allied troops' approach in 1814. The Tour de Paris, razed to the level of the curtain wall a few years earlier, was fitted with cannon, used to attack the rear of the allied troops during the combats at the eastern approaches to the capital in 1814. A cannon loophole was pierced in the centre of each of the two sections of the medieval enceinte north curtain wall: these alterations are probably the only surviving evidence of this Paris defensive system.
During the 19th century, some buildings were erected to meet the site requirements. Louis XVIII installed a unit of his guard at Vincennes and ordered the Pavillon des Armes to be built for them in 1819, one of the rare military constructions of that period surviving in France (classified as an historic monument). It houses part of the army history department archives and a reading room, open to the public.
During the Restoration period (1815-1830), the razing of seven of the nine medieval enceinte towers down to the level of the curtain wall was completed. Under the July Monarchy (1830-1848), "Building 6" was erected to house officers and, between 1832 and 1843, casemates capable of holding artillery – first elements of the Paris fortifications under discussion since the demise of the First Empire – were constructed against the medieval wall.
The casemates set against the south curtain wall, across the keep moat and against the north-west curtain wall, have now been demolished, but those which had been built against the north and north-east curtain walls and against the mantle wall♦ of the keep still exist.
The casemate located against the east section of the north curtain wall houses the air-force history department. Except for the archives consultation room, this building is not open to visitors.
After the defeat of 1871, highly typical military-style buildings, an architecture quasi-omnipresent in France of the period, were erected in the north half of the enceinte: the Pavillon du Harnachement and the structure now housing the Archives du Génie [Military Engineers Corps].

Left-hand page **Europe,** decoration glorifying Monsieur, Louis XIV's brother. Preparatory pen-and-ink sketch by Michel Dorigny for a ceiling in the Council Chamber of the Queen's Pavilion (Paris, MAP) and its execution on canvas (Paris, musée du Louvre).

♦***Mantle wall:*** *The masonry lining or casing of an enceinte serving to cover, protect, dress and reinforce it.*

The Tour des Salves, allowing communication between the castle or old fort and the new fort, after a postcard dating from the early 20th century (private coll.).

A short bibliography

Chapelot (Jean), *Le Château de Vincennes. Une résidence royale au Moyen Âge*, Paris, Éditions du CNRS/CNMHS, coll. "Patrimoine au présent", 1994.

Id., "Les résidences royales à l'époque de Philippe le Bel : ce que leur étude nous apprend sur ce règne", *1300. L'art au temps de Philippe le Bel*, Paris, École du Louvre, 2001, p. 33-74.

Id., dir., "Vincennes : du manoir capétien à la résidence de Charles V. Vincennes ; actualité de la recherche archéologique et architecturale", *Dossiers d'archéologie*, n° 289, décembre 2003-janvier 2004.

Id., "Les lambris du donjon de Vincennes (Val-de-Marne) : un rarissime témoignage du décor intérieur d'une résidence royale du XIVe siècle", actes des journées archéologiques d'Île-de-France, 30 novembre et 1er décembre 2002, Paris, ministère de la Culture et de la Communication, préfecture de la Région Île-de-France, direction régionale des Affaires culturelles, 2005, p. 57-76.

Chapelot (Jean), Lalou (Élisabeth), eds., *Vincennes, aux origines de l'État moderne*, actes du colloque de Vincennes, juin 1994, Paris, Presses de l'ENS, 1996.

Chapelot (Odette), ed., *Du projet au chantier. Maîtrise d'ouvrage et maîtrise d'œuvre aux XIVe-XVIe siècles*, Paris, Éditions de l'EHESS, 2001.

Consolidation et restauration du donjon de Vincennes, Paris, ministère de la Culture et de la Communication, Service national des travaux/Dominique Carré éditeur, coll. "Un chantier", 2007.

"Dossier château de Vincennes", *Monumental*, june 2006, p. 5-41.

Heinrichs-Schreiber (Ulrike), *Vincennes und die höfische Skulptur. Die Bildhauerkunst in Paris, 1360-1420*, Berlin, Dietrich Reimer Verlag, 1997.

Captions

Cover

Front: The keep and its enceinte, CMN/Caroline Rose.
Back: see p. 52.
Front flap: Angel, west portal of the palatine chapel, CMN/Patrick Müller.

Chronology

Left to right and top to bottom
- Political life: *Philippe Auguste*, MAP/AP. *Charles VII*, CMN/Jean-Jacques Hautefeuille. Emmanuel Frémiet, *Joan of Arc*, 19th century, CMN/Patrick Cadet. Anonymous, *François I*, wood, 16th century, Château d'Azay-le-Rideau, CMN/Patrick Müller. *Louis XIV*, Château d'Azay-le-Rideau, CMN/Patrick Müller. *Louis XV*, CMN/Acloque.
- Vincennes, principal dates: see pp. 5, 8, 50, 52, 61. Guardroom, King's Pavilion, CMN/Patrick Müller.
- Other royal residences: Guardroom, Palais de la Cité, Paris, CMN/Caroline Rose. Château de Saint-Germain-en-Laye, CMN/Patrick Müller. The Tuileries Palace after the fire, MAP/AP.

Photographic credits

CMN: Centre des monuments nationaux, Paris.
ERCVBE: Équipe de recherche sur le château de Vincennes et la banlieue est / CNRS/EHESS, château de Vincennes.
MAP/AP: Médiathèque de l'architecture et du patrimoine, Archives photographiques, Paris.
RMN: Réunion des musées nationaux, Paris.

Angers, musée des Beaux-Arts: 59 bl; Archives nationales: 5, 13; BnF: 8, 9, 10t, 14, 15t, 23, 46, 47, 58b; CMN/Philippe Berthé: 29c, 42b; CMN/Patrick Cadet: 48b, 50, 62t; CMN/Jean-Jacques Hautefeuille: 26b, 49, 60-61b; CMN/Patrick Müller: 2-3, 40t, 41b, 44b, 45ctl, 52t and b, 55, 57b, 59br, 60-61c; CMN/Caroline Rose: 22, 37t, 45tl, 53, 54, 56, 58t, 61c; CNRS Éditions/Patrick Charniot: 40b, 41t, 51; ERCVBE: 11, 15b, 17b, 25, 29b, 30-31, 32, 32-33b, 34, 36, 39, 42tr, 43b, 44, 45tr, ctr, c and b, 48t, 57t, 59t; Jean-Claude Golvin: 4, 20, 43; Jean-Jacques Hautefeuille: 7, 12, 16-17, 18, 19, 24-25, 26t, 52tl; P. Müller: 42tl; RMN: 27, 28, 40c, 61b; RMN/MAP/AP: 37b; Sceaux, musée de l'Île-de-France: 29t; Service historique de la Défense, archives de l'armée de l'air: inside front flap; Service historique de la Défense, archives de l'armée de terre: 6, 10b, 33t.

Collection director
Alix Sallé
Editorial coordinator
Mathieu Villard
Documentation coordinator
Dalloula Haiouani
Translator
Ann Sautier-Greening
Copy editor
Barbara Shapiro Comte
Production coordinator
Carine Merse
Graphic design
Atalante/Paris
Layout
Jean-François Gautier
Clara Desmet
Photoengraving
Scann'Ouest/Saint-Aignan-de-Grand-Lieu
Printing
Néo-Typo, Besançon, France

Dépôt légal: June 2005
Reprinted: September 2009

ISSN 1159-1722
ISBN 978-2-85822-843-0